the new

black

evie shockley

WESLEYAN UNIVERSITY PRESS

MIDDLETOWN, CONNECTICUT

the black unicorn

WESLEYAN POETRY

Wesleyan University Press

Middletown CT 06459

www.wesleyan.edu/wespress

© 2011 Evie Shockley

Manufactured in the

United States of America

Wesleyan University Press is a member
of the Green Press Initiative. The paper
used in this book meets their minimum
requirement for recycled paper.

Library of Congress Cataloging-in-Publication Data

Shockley, Evie, 1965–

The new black : poems / Evie Shockley.

p. cm. — (Wesleyan poetry)

ISBN 978-0-8195-7140-3 (cloth : alk. paper)

I. Title.

PS3619.H63N49 2011

811'.6—dc22

2010046345

5 4 3 2 1

This project is supported in part by an award
from the National Endowment for the Arts

NATIONAL
ENDOWMENT
FOR THE ARTS
A great nation
deserves great art.

for alicia and olivia,
the new blacks i love most

&

in loving memory of thelma lucille sayles clifton
(june 27, 1936–february 13, 2010),
in whose oceanic footprints
i splash, after

"i come to comfort the afflicted
and to afflict the comfortable"

All their stanzas look alike.

Even this, after publication,

Might look alike. Disproves

My stereo types.

Thomas Sayers Ellis

with the fate of a slingshot stone

loosed from the catapult pronged double with history

and time on a trajectory of hurl and fling

to a state active with without and unknown

i came upon a future biblical with anticipation

M. NourbeSe Philip

yes I've tried in vain

never no more to call your name

and in spite of all reminders

misremembered who I am

Harryette Mullen

contents

the cold

out with the new

the fare-well letters

black

my last modernist poem, #4
(or, re-re-birth of a nation)

a clean-cut man brings a brown blackness
to a dream-carved, unprecedented
    place. some see in this the end of race,

like the end of a race that begins
    with a gun: a finish(ed) line we might
finally limp across. for others,

    this miracle marks an end like year's
end, the kind that whips around again
    and again: an end that is chilling,
with a lethal spring coiled in the snow.

———————————

ask lazarus about miracles:
the hard part comes afterwards. he stepped
into the reconstruction of his
life, knowing what would come, but not how.

out with the old

my life as china

i was imported : : i was soft in the hills where they found me : : shining in a private dark
: : i absorbed fire and became fact : : i was fragile : : i incorporated burnt cattle bones'
powdered remains : : ashes to ashes : : i was baptized in heat : : fed on destruction : :
i was not destroyer : : was not destroyed : : i vitrified : : none of me was the same : :
i was many : : how can i say this : : i was domesticated : : trusted : : treasured : : i was
translucent but not clear : : put me to your lips : : i will not give : : i will give you what
you have given me

from The Lost Letters
of Frederick Douglass

June 5, 1892

Dear Daughter,

        Can you be fifty-three this
month? I still look for you to peek around
my door as if you'd discovered a toy
you thought gone for good, ready at my smile
to run up and press your fist into my
broken palm. But your own girls have outgrown
such games, and I cannot pilfer back time
I spent pursuing Freedom. Fair to you,
to your brothers, your mother? Hardly.

                      But
what other choice did I have? What sham,
what shabby love could I offer you, so
long as Thomas Auld held the law over
my head? And when the personal threat was
ended, whose eyes could mine enter without
shame, if turning toward my wife and children
meant turning my back?

                Your mother's eyes stare
out at me through yours, of late. You think I
didn't love her, that my quick remarriage
makes a Gertrude of me, a corseted
Hamlet of you. You're as wrong as you are
lucky. Had Anna Murray had your
education as a girl, my love for
her would have been as passionate as it

was grateful. But she died illiterate,
when I had risked my life to master language.
The pleasures of book and pen retain
the thrill of danger even now, and you
may understand why Ottilie Assing,
come into our house to translate me into
German, could command so many hours,
years, of my time—or, as you would likely
say, of your mother's time.

                    Forgive me,
Rosetta, for broaching such indelicate
subjects, but as my eldest child and
only living daughter, I want you to
feel certain that Helen became the new
Mrs. Douglass because of what we shared
in sheaves of my papers: let no one
persuade you I coveted her skin.
I am not proud of how I husbanded
your mother all those years, but marriage,
too, is a peculiar institution.
I could not have stayed so unequally yoked
so long, without a kind of Freedom in
it. Anna accepted this, and I don't
have to tell you that her lot was better
and she, happier, than if she'd squatted
with some other man in a mutual
ignorance.

           Perhaps I will post, rather
than burn, this letter, this time. I've written it
so often, right down to these closing lines,
in which I beg you to be kinder, much
kinder, to your step-mother. You two are

of an age to be sisters, and of like
temperament—under other circumstances,
you might have found Friendship in each other.

With regards to your husband—I am, as
ever, your loving father—

Frederick Douglass

celestial

—L.A., THE MID-1950S

her name was ella, *elle*, french for all woman,
everywoman, she, the third person, feminine,

hippy, buxom, regal curls piled atop her head,
soft shiny crown for her diamond voice, the soaring
swooping bird, the orchestra in her throat, the stars

in her eyes, the star in front of her eyes each night,
one week, at the mocambo, her name was norma,

she wasn't normal, blonde, her name was marilyn,
the *i* in angelic, first person, created, an immaculate

concept, the image of pure beauty, sound, power,
her name was ella, *elle* in french, all women,

in her, *i*'s, the star in front of her eyes, each night,
glamorous, first lady of song, iconic, backstage,
the effort behind the effortlessness, the exercise,

the training, the makeup that made up the woman,
her name was norma, marilyn, ella, *est-elle*, the star.

mesostics from the
american grammar book

we are the PROBLEM—the great national game of TABOO. — ANNE SPENCER

doro**T**hy dandridge
yellow ma**R**y peazant
h**A**lle berry
hel**G**a crane
mar**I**ah carey
Clare kendry

ma**M**a day
l**A**ni guinier
consola**T**a
zora neale hu**R**ston
an**I**ta hill
ntoz**A**ke shange
sapphi**R**e
ali**C**e walker
peac**H**es

saartjie b**A**artman
se**T**he

sall**Y** hemmings
n**O**la darling
maya angelo**U**
har**R**iet jacobs

jo**S**ephine baker
jan**E**t jackson
margaret ga**R**ner
Vanessa williams
desiree wash**I**ngton
sappho **C**lark
c**E**lie

statistical haiku
(or, how do they
discount us? let me
count the ways)

only 3 of 100 black boys
entering kindergarten will graduate college—
in the night sky, shooting stars

every day a black person
under 20 years old commits suicide—
plucked magnolia blossom's funereal perfume

a black man is 700% more likely
than a white man to be sentenced to prison—
scattered thundershowers in may

every 3 minutes
a black child is born into poverty—
pine needles line the forest floor

—after langston hughes's "johannesburg mines"

good   night   women
(or, defying the carcinogenic pen)

they are   :   *(like stars)*

rising

always brightly there behind our blindness,
pricking through the dark tent
with a fine, white rage
that burns garbage to ashes,
that fires truth to ceramic strength.

shining

beaconing us to a north we bring along
in our pockets, constellating,
andromedas fighting their own monsters,
dipping into history and wisdom,
filling to overflowing the big and little gourds.

falling

ripping hot and fierce down the night sky
till they are out of our pining sight,
too quickly, more frequently than we can bear,
their incandescent metal, incinerating, is
the occasion and inverse of wish.

—in memory of: audre lorde (1934–1992) / toni cade bambara (1939–1995) /
  sherley anne williams (1944–1999) / barbara christian (1943–2000) / claudia tate
  (1947–2002) / june jordan (1936–2002) / nellie mckay (c. 1933–2006)

her tin skin

i want her tin skin. i want
    her militant barbie breast,
resistant, cupped, no, cocked
    in the V of her elbow. i want
my curves mountainous

and locked. i want her
    arabesque eyes, i want her
tar markings, her curlicues,
    i want her tin skin. she
is a tree, her hair a forest

of strength. i want to be
    adorned with bottles. i
want my brownness
    to cover all but the silver
edges of my tin skin. my

sculptor should have made
    me like her round-bellied
maker hewed her: with chain-
    saw in hand, roughly. cut
away from me everything

but the semblance of tender.
    let nothing but my flexed
foot, toeing childhood, tell
    the night-eyed, who know
how to look, what lies within.

—after alison saar's "compton nocturne"

pink-think (a primer
for girls of other colors)

sunk in the pink of wealth: stinky in
    pink: rolling in bank that doesn't account
for an interest in violet. pink eye: not

a medical condition, but the ability to spot
    a good deal. pink rose, agency's paradox:
no passive princess: a pig for power.

powder puff? rare meat? half-moons, just
    above the cuticles, hover over pink squares
of terra firma. a pretty panther, stealing along

a sax solo on pink pads, gets down with
    the claws. mamí says, *if life hands you poverty,*
sell pink lemonade. yeah, mama says, *and*

    don't forget your tutu is a bishop, and winks.

clare's song

blonde fair bleached faded pale pastel light
blameless clean innocent guiltless pure clear
anatomy build figure person physique form
complexion countenance hue mien tint cast
bead dab dash ounce iota spot trace drop
succeed qualify answer do suffice suit pass

authorization permit ticket license paper visa pass
effortless facile moderate smooth undemanding light
abandon dismiss disown quit reject renounce drop
jump leap hurdle negotiate surmount vault clear
actors artists characters company players roles cast
behavior manner conduct custom practice rite form

arrange assemble concoct create devise forge form
cross depart flow go move proceed travel pass
copy duplicate facsimile mold plaster replica cast
amusing gay merry blithe pleasing witty light
accumulate gain acquire net realize secure clear
decrease decline downturn reduction slump drop

bleed dribble leak ooze seep splash trickle drop
character class grade make species variety form
audible lucid coherent distinct plain precise clear
canyon cut gap gorge path opening ravine pass
airy buoyant delicate feathery unsubstantial light
emit radiate diffuse spray spread scatter cast

appoint assign designate choose name pick cast
abyss chasm descent dip plunge precipice drop
angle approach aspect attitude slant viewpoint light

application sheet chart questionnaire blank form
advance overture proposition approach play pass
absolute convinced decided satisfied sure clear

bare empty free stark vacant vacuous void clear
boot fling heave hurl launch project toss cast
predicament crisis contingency plight state pass
collapse duck flop tumble pitch plummet drop
format framework order scheme structure form
beacon bulb dawn flash ray shine torch light

model pattern fashion form appearance contour cast
luminous radiant clear sunny ablaze aglow light
ebb fade wane depart drop end die decease pass

—after nella larsen

a sonnet for stanley tookie williams

won't you help to sing these songs of freedom?
'cause all i ever have: redemption songs.
— BOB MARLEY

all month this country has careened toward cold
and winter's celebrations: what a star
     announced—a birth—and then a chance to fold
a year away, pull one fresh from the drawer,

     if not clean, well, unworn. in just a few
months arrives the ice-hot day of the dead-
     come-back-to-life—time then to ask how new
and re- beginnings differ. mary bled

     for the december miracle, as some-
one must. did you imagine sacrifice
     as you called the crips to life? did they come,
those youngbloods, at the crackling of your voice,

     like lazarus to christ? vigilant night.
on the road to san quentin, candlelight.

(12/29/1953–12/13/2005)

17

in a
non-subjunctive
mood

if
i had
a dollar for

every
drop of
iraqi blood spilled,

every
woman raped,
every life destroyed

in this war,
i'd be
halliburton.

—*6/20/2007*

where's carolina?

east of childhood, north of
        capitol offenses, just west
   of a big blue treasure chest :
          wet coffin of neglected bones.
    in the veins, unnoticed as
a pulse. at a counter : sitting in
   varicolored eloquence. behind
         the mystery of the magnet. home
   of horton, poetry's bondsman :
     between anger and awe. below
the line, overrated, underestimated.
     helms territory : within a belt,
  an expanding waste. atop hades :
       persephone's threshold. beside
cloud-hooded mountains.
    outside time : a coltrane solo.
      far from fatal. after all.

x marks the spot

affable african

                                                            amiable american

affirmative african

                                              amazing american

affectless african

                                      ambulant american

affronted african

                                amorous american

affordable african

                          ambidextrous american

afflicted african

                      amusing american

affixed african

                  amended american

affirmative ambulance

amazing affront

           affordable amusement

ambidextrous affirmation

                affectless amateur

amiable affliction

                    affluent ambivalence

ameliorative affability

                      affected american

amenable african

                        african amendment

american afterglow

received in spring

a postcard   postmarked
from the snow-blanched mountains
of my before   its sloping
cursive recalls   *having*
funk   here you were wish

—for stéphane

the defense of marriage act,
alternatives to

act like you've seen breasts before
act like you can have sex when you get home
act like a commitment is a commitment is a commitment
act up
act like you want a wife, not a live-in nanny
act like you want a husband, not a sperm bank
act like you know a tax break when you see one
act right
act one: boy meets girl
act two: boy marries girl to her girlfriend
act three: boy attends 20th anniversary party for girl and her wife
act natural
act like this institution is more contractual than penal
act like you've heard of separation of church and state
act like you don't need a moat to define a marriage
act now

dependencies

visiting monticello was
an education   of course   you
named your home in a romance
language   spent 40 years
constructing it   and the myth
of yourself

we hold these truths

(freedom)

you designed your home on aesthetic
and scientific principles   maximizing   space
in the main house   by placing
the dependencies   beneath   and behind
it   built into the hillside   half
underground

to be self

*These "dependencies," or areas for domestic work, served as points of
intersection between Jefferson's family and enslaved people, and were
instrumental to the functioning of the house.*

-evident, that

i hear you loved
wine (we have that in common)
you had a cellar full of french
vintage you drew up
to the dining room   via
a dumbwaiter that ran between

you and the person
waiting (dumbly) below   to set
the dark bottles   in place

all men are

i hear you had
sally hemmings   i hear you
and she   had
six children   thus making a dependency
of your bedroom (another part
of the house   rarely seen)

created equal and are

(free)

you had james   (another
hemmings) to travel   to paris
to study french cuisine   to cook
for you   for wages
during your years in france

endowed

*Monticello, which means "little mountain" in Italian, was a house,
an ornamental landscape, a diverse community that included as many
as 140 enslaved men, women, and children, and a plantation.*

by their creator

as president   you sent lewis
and clark west   they returned
with maps   american elk antlers   native
american art painted on dried buffalo

hide   you placed
these items on your walls
for the edification of your visitors

with certain in alien able

you founded the university
of virginia   from your notes
students would learn they must compete
with the oorang-ootan   for
the negress's favors   from your life
they would learn

rights, that among

like you   i read   the poetry
of that good christian   phillis wheatley
her ode to george washington   the one
who freed his slaves

these are   life

you promised james hemmings
his freedom   if he would
return with you from france
(where he was   free) and teach   (enslaved)
others the french style of cooking
i hear   you were as   good
as your   word

liberty

*James Hemmings trained his brother Peter, completed an inventory of the
kitchen, and left Monticello in February 1796. Word came in 1801 that he
had "committed an act of suicide."*

and   [what was it locke said?]

your pen   successfully severed
religious belief   from civic life
you drafted the   declaration of   independence
this is the legacy   you left
to the country   to your creditors
you left   130 black people   enslaved
in payment of debts

the pursuit   of happiness

in some world   an even
newer one   i might have liked you
and you might have liked
(not fancied)   me
we might have shared   a bottle
a conversation   some poems
in this world   i prefer your   words
depending   on them   to be
better   than you

him/body/meant, her/body/meant

when i left home, i left behind the weight of failure.

in my desk chair, the cushions unforgiving of years of pressure, neck and spine aching,
    i stare into the screen,
try to forget my body, to fold it without wrinkles and tuck it away,
become eyes and brain.

i see bodies extended through technologies of touch,
the traffic in bodies,
the traffic of bodies, social choreography.

ah, frida, will you be better off when we've perfected the mechanics of the body?
the factory fuck. the bloodless baby.
get your ass on the assembly line.

the violence of social experience is not a sound i can represent with my palm, my fist.

lot was not the salt of the earth.
he was drunk.
he was raped.
we'll take his word for it.

when you walk away from home, look away. look aweigh. look: a way.

where you are planted

he's as high as a georgia pine, my father'd say, half laughing. southern trees
as measure, metaphor. highways lined with kudzu-covered southern trees.

fuchsia, lavender, white, light pink, purple : crape myrtle bouquets burst
open on sturdy branches of skin-smooth bark : my favorite southern trees.

one hundred degrees in the shade : we settle into still pools of humidity, moss-
dark, beneath live oaks. southern heat makes us grateful for southern trees.

the maples in our front yard flew in spring on helicopter wings. in fall, we
splashed in colored leaves, but never sought sap from these southern trees.

frankly, my dear, that's a magnolia, i tell her, fingering the deep green, nearly
plastic leaves, amazed how little a northern girl knows about southern trees.

i've never forgotten the charred bitter fruit of holiday's poplars, nor will i :
it's part of what makes me evie : i grew up in the shadow of southern trees.

a background in music

music city u.s.a. it was, nothing doing without a song,
    and not just twangy tunes that rhyme southern drawls
with guitar strings, though it's true i knew charlie pride
    before charlie parker, but music, music, music, broadway
numbers (*one!* . . .) broadcast over speakers in the park,
    pointer sisters fingering ohio players on the school bus,
the elementary chorus performing a patriotic medley
    for the bicentennial, the high school madrigals wringing
the *carol of the bells* out of our overworked throats each
    december, wvol simulblasting *car wash* or *little red corvette*
out the windows of every deep ride rolling in the black
    neighborhoods, melodies to carry over the clap*slap*snap
of our hands clocking time (*miss mar-y mack mack mack*)
    or to keep us out of trouble with the jump rope, pep squad
cheers to perfect, spontaneous spirituals in the church
    parking lot, and, yes, some country, the mandrells, the oak
ridge boys, tuning in to *hee-haw*'s banjo humor and gloom,
    the music was *howdy* and *whassup, hell naw!* and *aw yeah!*,
merry, happy, baby-baby, and *god loves you if no one else does*:
    to ourselves, to applause, in talent shows, in choirs, on cue
and (mostly) in key, we sang everything there was to say.

ode to my blackness

you are my shelter from the storm
                and the storm

my anchor
              and the troubled sea

       * * *

night casts you warm and glittering
upon my shoulders   some would
say you give off no heat   some folks
can't see beyond the closest star

       * * *

you are the tunnel john henry died
      to carve
i see the light
     at the end   of you   the beginning

       * * *

i dig down deep and there you are   at the root of my blues
you're all thick and dark, enveloping   the root of my blues
seem like it's so hard to let you go   when i got nothing to lose

       * * *

without you, i would be just

      a self of my former shadow

the cold

to see the minus

the ghost. the thing we could touch if its throbbing
absence were any more vast, any more like a molecule

of jupiter, all mass, weighing us down, but nothing
we can put a finger on. we squint to see the minus: water
take away holy, take away book, take away tree, take away

phantom limb, a connection our brains keep trying to make
with the dead and gone. minus family, minus portrait,

minus heirloom, minus hand-me-down, minus hand.
subtract the noise in the streets. subtract the streets. minus

keepsake, minus god's sake, minus evidence of things unseen:
the ghost. the thing we could touch if our throbbing

phantom limb really connected. our brains keep trying to make
sense of it. the life's work, the first or second generation's
at last accumulated wealth, undone by the wind, washed clean

away in polluted water. if ever there were ample space
for faith and despair, it is here. room enough to tackle a vision.

love life, with stitches

that's how we are in bed: all body and
raw with desire. the self we've somehow patched
    together is revealed, *voilà!*, as hand-
iwork, unhandily done: covers snatched

    back to expose ungraceful seams. we're arms,
reaching past the one who's holding us close
    to touch another, whose flesh, in turn, warms
to what it can't quite grasp. we're our own foes:

    januses, half-lost in longing or rank
nostalgia for some lover past or yet
    to come—anyone but the one whose flank
is pressed against ours: one mouth tastes the wet

    lips of *yes, now,* while our other mouth sighs
for an unsoft shoulder, unseeing eyes.

—*after louise bourgeois's* seven in bed

riven

i shift against the leather of my desk chair,
aware my back is off, awry, against me
    and the daily devotion i show to keyboard
and screen. my back makes its position
    clear. deep breathing discovers a depression—
in my mental image of this fickle body—
    right where my spine begins to dip, drains
it out only for pain's bitter juice to flood
    back in again. how much relief did frida
kahlo imagine she'd find in giving a brace
    responsibility for her back? how much did
she let herself taste? when does clamping
    down hard against certain unrelenting aches
begin to numb the senses indiscriminately?

my back tells me kahlo tacked her self-
portrait to canvas with oil to give herself
    nerve, nerves. no mirror, this painting reflects
what occupies her innards, what rives her
    so raggedly from chin to coccyx. she could
never bear—has forgotten how—to look
    as ripped apart as she feels, cannot afford
feeling. only with her artist's brush can she
    bead her face pearly and be open to flowing.
only that tool reveals her most distinct feature
    to be wings. she would fly the waste land
where her pain lives, if she weren't a pillar
    of civilization, weighted to earth by marble:
gray, sculpted, no less heavy for all its cracks.

—after frida kahlo's broken column

never after

was she enchanted, or drugged?
—HARRYETTE MULLEN

once upon a time, she went to a magical club on rush street, in chicago, illinois. she went with her girl, who went to pick up men. white men. her girl was a cinder ella. a goddaughter. wore the right shoes. a red cape with a hood. her girl knew a prince from a toad. and. how to get results. wolf whistles. she went to chaperone. she was the designated driver, especially when she drove home alone. she loved to watch the sun rise over the water, as she headed north on lake shore drive. she called her girl the afternoon after, to see how it went. to hear what went down. who went down. on whom. breakfast downtown, in some cool café. a ride home with the white knight in the morning in his imported, european steed. horsepower. she wasn't jealous. she had a man. a black man. she only wished she was invited to dance more at the club. she wasn't black enough. or. white enough. to catch the white guys' eyes. she didn't look like the type. to. she nursed her amaretto sour till it was mostly melt. she was the designated driver. the chaperone. the colored girl. whose skirt was not short enough or tight enough. to.

one night, her man was off from his job. parking steeds. imported, european steeds. for tips. for tuition. he could take her out. where? the magical club, downtown, on rush street, of course. she would not be a chaperone. she would be a princess. she would dance and dance. with her man. she would get down. on the floor. at the door, there was a problem. out of state ids. her id was from the same state it always had been. she was from out of state. her girl was from out of state. her man was from out of state. they were in college. they were seniors. they were legal. she made her case. she stood her ground. she put her foot down. on the one. on the two. they got in. paid the price. got their hands stamped. however. there was a pea beneath the dance floor. the clock kept striking midnight. she could not spin the straw into gold. she couldn't let down her hair. they knew it spelled trouble. but. they decided to have one drink and leave. they had a point to make. paid the price. drank the drinks. she ordered an amaretto sour.

they brought her a stepmother's special. a red delicious. they made their point. but. and. she pricked her finger on it. she began to fall. down. she could hardly stand. it. charming. her man's kiss did not revive her. make it go away. he carried her off into the set sun. off the set. up. she slept it off. they shrugged it off. they learned what they already knew. they knew better. they lived to tell the scary tale.

a matter of balance

it's not a goodbye fuck
unless you both know it.
this is a matter of balance.
if either of you is oblivious,
it's a dangling fuck—as with
syntax—one of you looking
forward to something
that simply isn't coming.

it's not a goodbye fuck
if it's not good. don't name
it—paint *love* and *forever*
silently on each other's skin
with amnesiac fingertips.
at its best, it is like having
your favorite meal, savoring
the sweet and salt, knowing

there's ground glass in
every bite. take in greedy
mouthfuls, eating till your
tongue is a beach, a raw,
glittering blanket of sand
with a red, metallic-tasting
ocean slowly overwhelming
the whole fucking thing.

on new year's eve

we make midnight a maquette of the year:
frostlight glinting off snow to solemnize
        the vows we offer to ourselves in near
silence: the competition shimmerwise

        of champagne and chandeliers to attract
laughter and cheers: the glow from the fireplace
        reflecting the burning intra-red pact
between beloveds: we cosset the space

        of a fey hour, anxious gods molding our
hoped-for adams with this temporal clay:
        each of us edacious for shining or
rash enough to think sacrifice will stay

        this fugacious time: while stillness suspends
vitality in balance, as passions
        struggle with passions for sway, the mind wends
towards what's to come: a callithump of fashions,

        ersatz smiles, crowded days: a bloodless cut
that severs soul from bone: a long aching
        quiet in which we will hear nothing but
the clean crack of our promises breaking.

the cold

—and after the panic,

          what?

the groaning of some
        machine meant to comfort us
the dry-eyed wakefulness
the work still to be done

where there's a whistle, there's
      a chill
where a sliver of light,   a poem

—that some morning we will push
     the earth   too far

will feel its bony elbow
                pushing back
will fall into it   as it caves in
     to our demands

under the moon's snow-stare
     at dumpsite
we should quake :: it's our fault

—the cold of a bomb crater
        radiates

through the smoking rubble
      of families
through scattered twigs :: young
        underfed lives

living and dead revisit together
the fruitless olive trees
           and prayers

—and after anticipation,
     where is   the body?

safely encased in marble
littered across
     contested   terrain
lips propped open ::   O

the footprints didn't sully
     the snow   until
they doubled   back

—as if tired of repetition   nature
                    veers off

hurricanes recalibrate our tolerance
            for wind and water
tsunamis chart new merritory
equatorial   muscles, nuzzles   polar

abnormal is the new natural
the flood next time   recycled
                    metaphor

—or nostalgia for one's ownly
                              culture

the draft from the window
          threatening to open
that said to be gone
                    but palpably upon one

goosebumps sweat blisters scabs
the body's outer layer
                    giving itself a way

—*ethical*   waved around
        like a wand

testifying to the bearer's magic
pointing always in opposite
        directions
the *i*   in *j'accuse*

ice clings thoughtlessly
                to saplings
aesthetics   stands in

—as the cold seeps up from the floor
      into my bones

can a feeling change a structure?
a pain departs
and do the bricks of the house
           lose their mortar?

a man opens his arms wide to the crowd
i read the gesture: *we*   i
    trace   the cross

out with the new

owed to shirley chisholm :

a nation outrageous in its hunger
for heart (not hearts) and enough sun-touching
    ladders to go around : hearty anger
unquenched by wet (american) (crutching)

    dreams, unmuted by the sound of rising
dough : yards of respect wrapped round her shoulders,
    more warming than fur because comprising
her due as a woman who ate boulders

    for breakfast, bravely : credit for having
an analysis of power sharper
    than sapphire's tongue, and props for behaving
like a natural woman, a world-shaper,

    who deserved a room—a trust—of her own :
the oval office : democracy's throne.

bop for presidential politics, c. 2008

it was a dark and nightly
storm. every whisker predictable,
predicted. the thunder drumming
against the usual lips and eyes,
the blood and bruises splitting
all the old familiar hairs.

it's gonna be a bright, bright, sunshiny day

deep beneath the ocean's surface
were the dead, the heavily equipped,
and the future. huddled around artificial lights
and repossessable voices, we
listened for the letters that corresponded
to our crusty belated sweet, but they were sandwiched
between other signals. the train kept starting
and stopping, unsure which year to be on time.

it's gonna be a bright, bright, sunshiny day

the rain made distinctions between land
and sea academic, so some professed to care
to know. *p* wasn't one of our letters, but it fell
frequently from above. technology
provided other views of the weather. our own
were muddy. murk was the new black.

here is the rainbow i've been praying for
it's gonna be a bright, bright, sunshiny day

getting around utopia

if you're like me, you
    closed your eyes one cool
        november evening, and opened
    them seconds later to see what
at last looked like. blurry,
    as through saline. bright, as
        through pupils (and minds)
    dilated. afloat on a sea
of ecstasy, you are shocked
    it's so hard to navigate. now
        that nearly anything on the boat
    can be an oar, it's as though
the cargo has all been tossed
    overboard. you may feel
        as if you've lost your bearings.

so blink a bit. now : look
    west. further. further. check
        the coast, where the joy is muddy,
    picking itself up from puddles,
where folks with lopsided
    smiles stare at rings stripped,
        not of meaning, but of status : that
    is california. now look closer.
closer. look to your left,
    to your right. as you'll see,
        california is the state of the nation.
    look familiar? keep looking,
however blinding the sun-
    shine. even when the load
        is light, witness is ours to bear.

you   can't deny it

cast of characters
speaker   an african american woman
you   an african american woman   →   *roster of emotions*
                                                      pride
                                                      puzzlement
                                                      connection
          setting: dinner, early 21st century   defensiveness
                                                       pleasure
                                                    understanding

                       selected bibliography: *annie allen*, brooks
                                              quicksand, larsen
wine: cabernet sauvignon, $10/glass   *the bluest eye*, morrison

                                    [blackens]

                                 style
        speaker: your hair   darkens   → ↕   you
                               texture

                                   [browns]

[enter *roster of emotions*, variously and all at once.]

        roster of emotions: [*at/on the table.*]   <u>historical allusions</u>
                                              1. rampart street
                                              2. harriet jacobs
                                              3. *a red record*
the ~~end~~ _____   4. b.a.m.
        a. same old story   5. *vogue*
        b. continuing saga   6. etc.
        c. fuck?, what
        d. possibilities for new developments should be nurtured, as should the souls
            of *speaker* and *you*
        e. script!, flip/rip/skip/slip/encrypt

                   (to be acted [upon])

womanish

they are both the me i wish i'd been
      at their age: tween avatars of the two
personas i alternate like a hologram.
      the girl on the left is drenched in
rainbows, even in a black & white:
      colors arc across her t-shirt: her bead
necklace, button earrings, and fabric
      bow-rette are a candy-coated clutch

on childhood. big white plastic shades
      melt her eyes into the chocolate of her
skin: blonde braids streak through
      thin individuals pulled up and back
from her face then left to swoop
      towards her chin. the v of her fingers
leans on its side—a gesture that shows
      how dope and mellow she is, but also

puts a cat on the edge of her glasses.
      no curve breaks her mouth's cool
plane. behind and to her right, her
      alter ego (and mine) pushes her lips
up beneath her nose and lets her cheeks
      rise on her cheekbones, as her sense
of mischief draws a parenthesis around
      her smile and shines out of her eyes,

unhidden. she's graduated to bling,
      gold chain hanging over a worn collar,
a thick textured ring bright on the finger
      beside the one she gives the photo-

grapher: as generous as her friend is
reserved. *don't fuck with us*, they both
signal, impassive pacifist and trickster
of self-defense. *we'll take care of you.*

—*after* Youngin's Giving Up Peace and the Finger
(Washington, D.C.), TSE 2007

duck, duck, redux

those who cannot remember the past are doomed to repeat it. —GEORGE SANTAYANA
those who cannot forget the past are destined to remix it —ME

*this is the way we wash our face, wash our face, wash our face, this is the way we wash
our face, so early in the morning.* this is the way we segregate our schools in 1896. this
is the way we segregate our schools in 2007. *mary had a little lamb,* a bad, bad black
sheep with three bags full of wool. *it followed her to school one day, work one day,
wimbledon one day, it followed her to church one day, which was against the rule.* this
is the way we patrol the roads in the antebellum south. this is the way we patrol the
streets in our shiny new york. cue wedding bell. *oh bring back my sean-y to me.* this is
the way we appropriate black culture in the post-reconstruction period. this is the
way we appropriate black culture in the 21st century. *this little piggy went to market,*
got mad bling for spittin wack rhymes and calling women hos, and still wound up
crying *we, we, we, all the way home.* this is the way we use a noose in jim crow
america. this is the way we use a noose in jena, louisiana. *little blues boy, come blow
your horn.* i'm sorry to tell you, but his horn's done gone, and as for the boy who
used to blow so sweet, he's under a mountain of debt, working for minimum wage.
*this is the way we wash our hands of you historically, throw you into the atlantic,
spray you with birmingham hoses, this is the way we wash our hands of you today,
with jerry-rigged levees, so early, so so early in the millennium.*

because there should be love

there should be love poems. iridescent odes to skies
and their fluid, mutating blues, their restless canvases

where we cast the adjectives—*brilliant, dark, deep, clear*—
that name our daily moods, ringing doubt and delight,
confusion and cheer, the brave lines we spit to spin

out the re-newed story of two lives winding themselves
into joy. there should be lyrics that hit all the notes—*do,*

mi, sol—in the scale, that belt them out as they arrive—
passionate, pushy, pulsating, unpredictable—breathing

the whole—*billie, abbey, ella*—range of the torchlit heart.
there should be love poems, star-sprung stanzas that try

out the rough ballad of two lives lifting themselves
higher together than apart: that sing it: breaking relief,
each waking, that the hours are ours to share: certainty

that silver-lines even cumulonimbus ire: the *your hand*
in my hand in your hand of right now, and from now on.

—for l.c. & t.r.

improper(ty) behavior

racial profiling: the idea that there's no legitimate reason for driving while black.
take sean bell: he got 50 bullets pumped into his car for driving while black.

homeownership is also improper behavior, in cambridge and beyond.
ask henry louis gates—arrested in his own home for thriving while black.

seemed like the obamas' celebratory fist-bump might derail his campaign.
now they know they should avoid things like high-fiving while black.

inner-city hoops are, of course, appropriate—unlike swimming in the suburbs.
the *creative steps day camp* kids were booted from a pool for diving while black.

even b-ball can fall out of bounds, if the finals pit you against a whiter team.
the rutgers women's players were slammed on the air for striving while black.

post-katrina new orleans is open to anyone with the money to rebuild—
except the 9th ward, which they're discouraged from reviving while black.

it's all about belonging: even now, who belongs where is often based on who
belonged to whom. i sometimes wonder how i get away with living while black.

at the musée de l'homme an exhibit called *femmes du monde* is

on display(ed) legs shaved vulvas announce *no peace no pussy* from
la city of angels one imagines that beneath their light blue chadris the
women of afghanistan are also as bare as the day they were borne bearing psy-
chic scars after cleansing the darfurian refugees the hutu the tutsi they cover with
floral scarves wrap themselves in fabric bearing the words *stop the violence against women*
did she or the photographer who pays *his women* the going european modeling rates choose
to position this printed protest across her derrière apropos of the brazilian-cut bikinis of women
in cali and sao paulo *les femmes* as tourist attractions mutilations cut the pleasure of african women
in half but afford the men of the museum another opportunity to view the clitoris disappearing like
saartjie baartman's at long last the smile of the indigenous tahitian woman who comes right out of a
gaugin with lips and breasts plumping round and firm from her youthful body decorated with painted
designs as intricate as the hairstyles the mauritanian twins in nouakchott change like costumes to
match their moods like the messages on the t-shirts of the all-girl punk band in beijing screaming in
english *have rock* and *deeds not words* from passion to politics and the critique the aboriginal aus-
tralian artist spits of the white man(her broker)'s greed demanding more than 50 percent of the
selling price of her works because it's his market and her/their/women's place in it is lying on a
bed on a cot on a mat on the floor always horizontal be they lawyers soldiers princesses pros-
titutes actors activists or acrobats on five continents in dozens of countries in the world
the women are lying down down for the men the men of the many museums museums
that bring them back to the drawing board and hold them still for the camera the
visitor the voyeur the man even the woman of the north-south-east west
who will leave this exhibit feeling at best equal parts desire and dis-
gust for the sad and sexy and vulnerable and plaintive and open
and apathetic and inviting and inaccessible and
yours for the taking as book or dvd

a question of survival

are we defined   by what we   can survive or   what we can't?   some of us
     can test toxins   on colored orphans :   can ask them   to swallow what
their bodies will   reflexively push up   or down and   out until their
     muscles clench around   the memory of   water and their   limbs thin and
tremble like twigs   in winter. some   of us can't.   some of us   can learn to
     gulp down drugs   before we're old   enough to spell   f.d.a. — while still
too small and   silent to be   considered consenting : can   drink exotic cocktails
     and live to   teach the doctors   a thing or   two about dosage.   and some of
us can't. what   would darwin say?   ask miss evers.   ask her boys.

soundtrack for a generational shift

you may have no knowledge of musical things, but . . . — THE SUPREMES

deep into our visit, after i've adjusted the head of your bed down, up, and back
down again, i offer you my ipod. two weeks too early, the twins dance
inside your cupola of a belly, moves a cross between the electric slide and a toyi-toyi
of protest. singing our old favorites has only egged them on. the budding aunt in
me thinks, *we need a lullaby.* the closest i've got: alice coltrane's vedic jazz. earbuds in,

you rest your head against the pillows and let your eyelids drop. how often
have i seen this you: teresa in repose. the eternal plastic curlers in your hair have
created their familiar green halo. you're 7 and my weary co-conspirator in
a plot to stay awake past bedtime : you're 22 and doggedly ignoring a midnight
melody of manhattan sirens : but, suddenly, 39 and trying not yet to give birth,

you're more than you : i see the visages of our mother, her father, their cheekbones,
the nose of our father's mother, and more, shifting over your face, as if you'd become a
composer of genealogies, practicing the twins' potential features on your own.
of course, the palimpsestic show closes before i can identify all those—the dead and
the living—who've traversed the room to bless our impending transitions. *i sorta like that
song,* you concede, graciously. *the harp is beautiful, but* you can't stand the saxophone
that reminds you of our father, practicing his while we were supposed to be asleep.
my effort to calm the girls has riled you a bit, but they seem distinctly serene. the
heart monitors chart a less ragged graph, and you finally relax as the computer
sings a decrescendo of beeps. rest now. nocturnal rehearsals of a new duet start soon.

revisiting

i was waiting on a poem when

my grandfather pushed through the screen

door, the wire-webbed rectangle left

slapping the wooden jamb behind him. i had

not seen pop too often since he'd died,

hadn't let my mind zap through the gray

distance from my cool, bright here-and-

now back to the porch where, as a girl, i'd

waited out tennessee evening heat

cradled in the suspended swing. down

the dingy white cement stairs, across

the dirt yard along a track made in

part of rusting sheets of scrap metal

and part embedded flat-top stones pop

goes, turns left at the road, and shambles

through the pasture gate to call the cows.

sook, cows, sook, sook. their lowing answers

him. they flick their ears, push themselves

up from their knees, come like dignified

dogs to follow him in a procession

to the barn. with fist-sized onyx eyes

and patternless black and white markings,

they pick their way over uneven

turf on precise hooves. he pens them, then,

tossing loose straw over the rails with

a free hand. he has come back to me

at 70—young as i ever

knew him—wearing his old baggy pants

and wattled triceps, but still able

fields each morning. now, his p.m. chores

swinging his leg out and over like the arm

the mule trods the gravel road up from barn

after the war—that and a life-sized

pop turned her forty into hundreds.

a head for figures surprised nearly

to saddle up and ride to the corn-

at the barnyard done, he mounts,

of a neglected compass. *gee up.*

to stable. pop's momma got a mule

plot of land. one of the lucky ones.

black man with a few years of school and

everyone but himself. home again

from the stable, pop's boot soles molt mud

my grandmother comes back to me, too,

it dries. i straddle the two worlds: in

the swing, fat toes callusing against

the tired beam holding me aloft

easy silence that fell between us:

old eyes able to spot contentment

on the porch. it'll stay there unless

this evening, to whisk it away when

one, my seven-year-old legs motor

the dusty floor planks they barely reach,

creaking loud enough to fill the half-

in the other, my thirty-three-year-

in pop's. he is pleased to perform this

evening ritual with his youngest

of his pipe in the bowl of his palm,

daughter's girl for company. the bowl

pop pries open the red prince albert

tobacco tin, tips out a tiny

ration of the brown ground and tamps it

into the pipe's hollow, his work-thick

finger just the right size to fit. quick

hiss of sulfur-scented flame and he's

drawing peace from poison, blowing sweet

aroma towards me like a misty

kiss, rocking in the thin, paint-bare arms

of his old throne, watching the late sun

melt into the branches of his trees.

—for leatha

her table mountain

every poet has a table mountain tucked right beneath epidermis,
waiting for the prick of evening wind for release. — P.G.

they'd been to the same city, but you wouldn't have known it. he came home
blissing about jacaranda in bloom; on her visit, winter hid

color behind the thick gray of clouds and rain, except for those pastel
houses hiking up the steep slopes of the bo-kaap, a little squint-and-

see-san-francisco quarter early muslims had raised like a garden
in the town. he sang in liquid tones of how the atlantic reached down

and crooked her blue finger round this lucky cape before giving the sea-
bed over to the indian ocean. she recognized that body,

too, instinctively: there, the same wet cradle and grave it was where she
knew it best—but there it was also jailer and jail, cruel cup in which

rose the knuckle of land where mandela and sisulu couched their hopes
across an ignorant count of years. his table mountain was a vast,

gentle lover. *i spent the clearest night of my life on its summit.*
all the universe was caught up in my throat. she recalled her ascent.

the cable car, as it lugged itself from high to heights, twirled her once
around in a slow, careful dance across the sky. even gray, the views

were punctured with beauty: the steel blue bars of ocean rolling into
the waterfront; buildings pushed unpredictably into parallels

or angles with each other—like a jar of pearly rectangular
buttons spilled, splayed, and then swept into a haphazard constellation—

arrayed from water to mountain base and out onto the flats in an
endless shimmering; the craggy stone of the mountain face foreboding

an unforgiving terrain. she spent the coldest afternoon of her
life on that summit, coatless in thirty-degree winds, her numb fingers

cramped around her camera, ankles turning on the trail's uneven
rock. between billows of mist, she gazed down into a city that tried

to cut out its own heart—it still bore the grassy scar where district six
had thrummed—and she loved it: utterly, open-eyed, as fiercely as if

it were hers or herself, despite the miserable august weather,
despite the acid tang she detected in his *place of sweet waters*,

despite the history of peoples chained and chaining, killed and killing,
that hung over it like the clouds over that prehistoric mountain.

notes to my nieces (or, essays in fortune-telling)

when i was younger, trees
were green, money was green, money
grew on trees, or trees grew up
and became money. now, money is clearly
plastic, spreads like cancer, getting it
is genetic.

trust me on this. *g o d* stands
for *good old days*, and if you have enough
faith, you can remember them almost
like you were there, on your knees
with us, scrubbing them clean or
praying for the millennium, that next life,
when the *g o d* would be *n e w* : *not*
especially white.

question: your
mother is black and your father is loving.
answer: what's loving got to do
with virginia?

i fear
that your cows ain't like mine, that you
won't understand why i gave up
red meat.

say the past is a muddy
river. say the future is a belated alphabet
with which you and i might spell
different things. say the present
is something we can pass back and forth
between us, like an acorn, like
loose change.

coming of age

until i turned thirteen   until that afternoon in
the locker room when i heard you sing *soft and wet* from beginning to
end   so sweetly relentless i forgot to be shy about the half-nakedness
of my awkwarding body   paused with musky gym shorts in hand while
time slipped into your drum machine   and rivered over your keyboards

i'll bet i'd never heard a boy
be so damn   accurate   about the state of my titillation   and be cause
there was your voice   *cream*   to dive into   to ladle out in long thin threads
for   (*purple doves   i wanna be delirious*)
you   (*little red kiss   if i was your erotic city*)

you sang   for me   for us   the holy promise of your shadowed eyes was my
own and my best friend's daily church   long phone calls from darkened rooms
my *head* between your hi-fi croon and her whisper   we sang   for   the whole
heart of our friendship pulsed with   *do me, baby*   with   *still waiting*
and why we needed to see   be   the reflection of your *dirty*
mind in   for   each other   for all those hot years

i still do not know   we talked of other boys   learning how desires of   for
truly woman bodies could be spoken   from a man's falsetto   what it is to
adore sex   a prayer for flesh to meet flesh like a thundercloud   *soft*
you sang   and sing still today in my own and my lover's skin   *and wet*

go-go tarot

u-haul yourself up by your bootstraps might be the fortune this photo tells for the youngblood sitting loose-legged on the tail of a mostly empty rental truck with plates from arizona, a state of confusion that doesn't see a day's worth of celebration in the life of dr. king, that mistakes mccain for a maverick. but he is—no, *you are* in d.c., and no matter how hot your future gets, or how it gets hot, it will not be a desert, so i'll search for other signs. i

around the heel giving them the look of spats, you are surrounded by potential portents. could be the goddess of those shoes will bless or curse you with game, will guide your feet easily or let you get tripped up among the many cords snaking along your path. a full heritage of afro-forward music-making, symbolized by the dj's pulpit, is yours by birth to earn—but the inverted reading focuses on the dj himself, squarely, yet barely,

stop speaking *of* you, to speak *to* you, once my eyes fall into yours staring somberly, directly, at the camera. you, little man, handsome already at eight years old, dwarfed by the massive stack of stereo equipment beside you—players, receivers, amplifiers, spewing wires as thick as hoses and thin as an unemployment check, all crowned by a mixer wide enough to dance on—you, sporting fresh white kicks, black rubber coating on the toe and

in this shot, all but concealed (there's a corner of his tee, a leg of baggy denim) behind his instruments, as if to say that you, too, could become an invisible man. well, no. not on my watch. if i'm reading this card (i'm reading this card), it's not *the tower,* it's *the world.* look at you, perched on the threshold, the door wide open. with *university* fixed across your chest and a pair of drumsticks in your hand, you've got everything you need to beat the odds.

—*after* Son of Backyard
(Washington, D.C.) TSE 2008

quiet as it's kept

no one tells you about these boys : their quiet feminism
grows like wildflowers : in their mothers' gardens : you
should take a field

                  trip : i'm telling you : they are

                            like

architectural flourishes

            unseen

                all about town : baroquing
libraries : finishing museums with clean modern lines : no
one tells you not to look past neat

                  in search of

                     shine
or brawn : the masculinity that winks and whistles at you
like times

         square or roars and kicks up dust like a pick-up
truck : the open

           secret of such sexiness has its charms :
but the boys who hold doors for men and women : who
catch you watching them adjust

              their glasses and

                  eye you
a smile : no one tells you what such quiet signs can mean
: i'm telling you that these boys

             flowering

              flourishing
and their dancing-star eyes can spark enough heat to warm
you through a massachusetts winter : pools of melt making
mud of your footprints : behind you

              the ice freezing silently

over your private spring

tonight i saw

lynn whitfield smile

it was like an audacious plethora of egalitarian embers signaling *agape*
it was like a brazilian bonfire leaping towards a jewelicious blanket of heaven
it was like a crew of fairies cascading from the dreams of an iridescent hummingbird
it was like a dozen jasmine-scented candles encircling the passionate pillows of ossie
        davis and ruby dee
it was like an ella fitzgerald rendition of *take the "a" train* slinging all the nyc subways
        into orbit along the rings of saturn
it was like 49 icelandic hot springs spraying the bright sky of a white night
it was like genuine a-1 pure-d baby's breath solidified puff by tiny puff and bunched
        together in a cluster

it was like a hearty slice of coltrane's *naima* solo suspended in air by a grace note
it was like the inky delight incandescing in her eyes
it was like a josephine baker banana skirt in a world where there had never been a
        banana republic
it was like kangaroo-high jumping as the expression of hooray by a host of gooseberry-
        flavored kindergarteners
it was like the light that shimmies outrageously down the aisle on easter sunday in
        4-inch heels and a feather-bedecked crown
it was like the manx's missing tail curled up and tickling the chin of an infant
it was like a new declaration of independence applicable globally and sung by a
        choir of bodacious bracelets
it was like 100 neon sunflowers blooming in a new moon november
it was like a polar icecap reflecting the milky way for the amusement of soulful life
        in andromeda

it was like a quest for unruly rubies leading to a glowing molten lava-capped
        mountain peak
it was like rivers of auroras coursing toward the equator on the midnight winds
it was like the sudden silver-velvet of her voice

it was like the triumphantly climactic intercourse between a hallelujah button and
a funkadelic holey-moley
it was like an unintimidated brassiere parade alive with brassy ballads reclining upon
brazen floats
it was like a vertiginous wingspan of ecstatic diamonds emerging from the earth of
their own accord

it was like whiskey distilled with water collected from eyes harriet tubman had just
shown canada
it was like xylophone tones vibrating up and down zora neale hurston's spine until
she momentarily explodes into legible confetti
it was like *yes* spelled out in 39 languages using tulip tiaras and halogen bulbs across
a clearing near a rainforest
it was like a zoological exploration of the sun that discovered the true source of all
that fabulific nurturing brightness

lynn whitfield's smile

salty (extended play)

i find you embedded in the earth permeating it like salt

you add a fine white spice to my diet like salt

at night you glisten the hot surface of my skin like salt

you send my blood pounding through my arteries like salt

you stick to my fingers until i lick you off like salt

at my feet you crumple into a little spill of bad luck like salt

you symbolize the gritty edges of my outrage like salt

i grind you into my wounds and you bite like salt

explosives

a	bomb	is a	statement	a	poem
a	bomb	is what a	statemeant	a	poem
				a	poem
the pleasure		of your	mental	energy	
		your	statementality	is a	poem
		a	state	makes	
a	bomb	makes a	state(ment)		
		the sent i	meant		
	bomb	is	(st)ate	you ear	
				you heard	
drop a	bomb	on em			
			state	your	
stop the	bombing				
		your	state		
the			state	in	
		your	state	of disarray	
		what a	state	we're in a	poem
a	bomb shelter				
		from the	statement	storm	
she's a	bombshell	in a	state	of	po(em)
		your	state	of mind	
				please repeat	
stop	bombing	your closing	statement		
				dis	poem
da	bomb			dis	poem
to blow up					

is a	question
is a	quest
	requests
isn't it	
a	request
of the	
the	question
	request
	question
you can't	question
we	request
a	sequester
ver(i)ty	
	question
your	request
is	
is about	

(mis)takes one to know one

i dreamed i told frederick douglass
        barack obama isn't black. not yet
the gray elder statesman, in the shape
        he assumes for oneiric work, he gave
me the look that covey surely took
        with him to his grave: direct metal
to match the channel carved between
        his brows, the cheekbones driving
up toward decision-making. *the child*
        follows the condition of the mother? don't
mix up servitude with race. i would think
        the president of the united states could
not be a slave to anyone or anything
        except his own desires. but black? answer
this: what is the story your president tells
        of his life? that is the question. always,
some among us have chosen to be or
        not to be what laws or customs inscribe
in our blood. race is not biology: it is
        the way the wind blows when you enter
a room, how you weather the storms,
        how you handle being becalmed. black,
white, red—colors, symbols, myths. i
        never knew a white parent to stand
between a colored man and his destiny.

        pshaw! he rebutted my cocked eye-
brow. *don't tell me times have changed!*
        of course they have! i saw so much
change in my lifetime, some days i lost
        my breath in the drag winds off worlds
hurtling into history. when i was a lad,

you'd never have convinced me white men
would kill white men by the hundreds
                of thousands freeing the negro—even as
the desperate, calculated means to purely
        economic ends. exhaling outrageously,
he adjusted the vest around his barrel
            chest and relaxing waistline. *but war*
came and, in its wake, amendments—
    if not amends—were made. seven years
after its end, i was running for vice-
            president of the union. no, the equal rights
ticket didn't win, and it only took
        another one hundred and thirty-six years
to put a colored man in the white house.
            i saw the steel in his eyes glimmer—
or glint. *your president will be what*
        his country has taught him to be, will
do what his experience leads him to do.
            don't mix up change with progress.

post-white

my country tears of thee sparkling on a stiff gray bow tied against cognitive dissonance
getting a)head holding it together keeping it really warm sweet land of basketball
barbeque sweet potato pie and cadillac liberty crowned lady with a torch in her voice
of(f thee i spring hopeful at last my love you've come a long way baby on the stony road
we trod through this land where my fathers and mothers died on poplars in quarters
under the lash and over the objections of the vocal few singing freedom oh freedom
over me and the authors of declarations of independence finally appointed to positions
of authority phillis wheatley with pen in hand and internationally recognized skill in
diplomacy secretary of state frederick douglass who won't dread scott's claim of
citizenship chief justice of the supreme court harriet jacobs master strategist speaker
of the house music moving mountains i'd let freedom ring with the harmonies of liberty
a work song hold it steady right there while i hit it reckon you oughta get it a tisket a
tasket we drop-kicked that old basket mama's got a brand new bag and say it plain
from that day forward we were all hip hop you don't stop being american

the fare-well letters

the fare-well letters

dear ace bandage,

    the wound is hard to place.
the wound is not your job.
    i thought i needed you, but
things are already tight. you
    are like putty in my hands,
or is my thinking colored?
    flesh tone or dial tone? who
you gonna call? your pretty
    silver broach sets in, holds
you at a tension. could it
    clasp the skin together long
enough for two flaps to re-
    attach? miss match. rematch.
love. ace. deuce. game. open.

         *

dear cuddly dharma,

you make it easy to say no,
just. i turn a blind eye to
temptation after staring hard
into your hydrogen smile. we
spoon, and i hate to stir, but
fetish is always in the mix.
even fate looks glamorous
by lamplight. spotlight. hot.
wound or would? would or
wooden? batter batter batter!
you have a dream of night-
marish proportions. where
there's a will, there's aweigh.
unanchored. unmoored. off.

*

dear existential fallacy,

i need you to be concrete.
you need me to liquidate
     my account. pour, pour me,
with my fluid tale. tail, to
     hear you tell it. fluent in six
currencies. dirty lucre. you
     tracking bills counterfeited
by the page. lyre, lyre, pants
     the town crier. griot. seer.
sikh. psyche. that, baby, went
     out with the dirty dishwater.
cross my palm with olives:
     i will tell you your pastime.
your passive voice is dated.

*

dear gift horse,

open wide. now bite down.
that incident was not an
        accident. don't. act like i'm
stupid. do you come with
        a saddle? which way to
the sunset? that's the thing
        about possibility: it's dark
in there. you can't judge
        an r&b song by its covers.
colors. dolores is blue: why
        must she give up her security
blanket? she's had it since
        she was born. my, what sharp
teeth you have! all the better.

*

dear ink jet,

black fast. greasy lightning.
won't smear. won't rub off.
defense: a visual screen: ask
an octopus (*bioaquadooloop*).
footprints faster than a speed-
ing bully, tracking dirt all
over the page. make every
word count. one. two. iamb.
octoroon. half-breed. mutt.
mulatto. why are there so few
hybrids on the road? because
they can't reproduce. trochee
choking okay mocha. ebony,
by contrast, says so much.

*

dear kerosene lamp,

i thought i'd put you behind
me. you're still there, back in
the day, but casting your glow
into my future. casting call.
cattle call. who you gonna
call? what gets you fired up?
a decent fuel. feud. food
for thought: wiki, wiki, wiki,
wiki. i carry a torch for you.
daytime décor, nighttime
necessity. curiosity. dare we
step beyond your radiant
radius, holy? wholly? anti-
quated. the way we live now.

*

dear mid-afternoon nap,

allow me. no, after you. to
take a break and make it.
    last, forever. what's up with
the pointy ears? what planet
    are you from? questions as
old as the stars. scars. slurs. we
    go boldly into new worlds, all
our expectations intact, no new
    ideas: secret hopes of meeting
our own warped selves in poor
    disguise. gauzy. hazy. who's
he? you. me. wake up, wake up,
    whenever you are! mourning
bells. hear? ring, rang, wrong.

*

dear opaque policy,

transparency is the new *this
is for your own good.* covering
   your ears is a sound defense.
the status quo never looked
   so good. goods. and servers.
ye gods! the national security
   blanket is a crazy quilt. award
awash aweigh awol. a globe
   warming up to consumption.
he's got the whole world in
   his lands. friends. ends. trust
me. must we? survey says:
   property. and life, and liberty,
but only if you're not it. tag.

*

dear quaalude residue,

you left a coating of many
colors along the walls of my
    veins. bloodstream. main-
stream. settle down. it's no
    game, this trivial pursuit of
happiness. are we there yet?
    when reality doesn't go down
easy, take something that will.
    what are we waiting for? i'm
shaken, but not stirred. who
    cares? shares? tears cloud our
eyes. billows. borrows. wheel-
    barrows, red, and full of white
chickens. now you can rest.

*

dear safety test,

do not pass go. do not pass
on. do not collect goose eggs.
don't risk it all. resistance is
fertile. fragile. versatile. can
you steal home? can you steal
away? we need results. you
need dummies. let's make
a wheel. again. from the be-
ginning. the skin is the first
layer of defense. if this were
a real emergency, you would
receive an s o s. calling all
black folks. come in. come out.
ready or not. i ain't got long.

*

dear untimely violet,

i doubt you. or your rich hue.
your sturdy whisper has no
    credibility in the era of pre-
cautionary bombing. greed
    wants war. need fights it.
bread for ammo. sent for you
    yesterday. here comes trouble.
come *n* trouble. hits like a
    glove (boxes). fits like a love
(clings). rhymes with trigger—
    and don't neither one mean
no good. i'd rather the bullet.
    go on. pull it. afraid? chicken
sticks. names will never let go.

*

dear white xmas,

    cross my heart. heat. hurt. an
insulting injury. the wound
    is hard to place. oh. *ou?* x marks
the spot. spooky. 'tis the sea-
    son to be haunted. attached
to the past. in the grip of ships.
    ahoy! unmoored. a pale ailment.
hail and well met. meant well.
    enough. frothy, snow-capped
waves. an icy greeting. a cold
    snap. slap. slip. a lightmare,
lightly whipped. screamy. hissy.
    fit to be tied. a tempered tantrum.
just like the ones i used to throw.

          *

dear yesterday's zero,

you were a beacon of just-
is. an iron maiden carrying
a dark torch, you're off for
tomorrow's equation with a
long-fixed formula: the some
is greater. here's a new math,
maybe involving less division.
a chance to set a light out for
the territories. suited you to
a tee, to sink a whole in one.
e pluribus the same old *unum*.
today the game has changed.
new rules. you've met your
match. score, for now, love all.

notes

celestial: Not long ago, I was surprised to learn that Marilyn Monroe, a huge fan of Ella Fitzgerald, had used her star power to knock Jim Crow out of the way of the jazz singer's own rising star. This poem and two others ("to see the minus" and "because there should be love") are all in the form called "the gigan," invented by Ruth Ellen Kocher.

mesostics from the american grammar book: With gratitude to Hortense Spillers. The epigraph is taken from Anne Spencer's self-authored bio in *Caroling Dusk: An Anthology of Verse by Black Poets of the Twenties*, edited by Countee Cullen (p. 47).

dependencies: The italicized text is quoted verbatim from the brochure I was given as a visitor to Monticello in April 2009.

statistical haiku (or, how do they discount us? let me count the ways): Statistics taken from "What Can We Do?" by Marian Wright Edelman, in *How to Make Black America Better* (2001), as well as university studies and U.S. governmental agency reports published between 1993 and 2005.

him/body/meant, her/body/meant: Lines from the stanza referencing Frida Kahlo are drawn from an exercise in which I collaborated with Amy Chavasse, who teaches in the Dance Department at the University of Michigan, and Aimee Meredith Cox, now my colleague at Rutgers, teaching in the African American and African Studies Department on the Newark campus. The exercise was part of a workshop in the Touching Time: Bodies/Writing/History practice-based research symposium held at the University of Michigan in April 2008.

bop for presidential politics, c. 2008: The italicized refrain for this bop was drawn from "I Can See Clearly Now," by Johnny Nash. The version playing in my head was recorded by Gladys Knight and the Pips (1973).

you   can't deny it: In the early-to-mid-1800s, on one side of New Orleans' Rampart Street lay the French Quarter and on the other, "the frontier." Congo Square was on the outside of Rampart Street, north of the French Quarter. Rampart was also well known as the street on or near which many white men kept houses for their octoroon concubines.

because there should be love: This epithalamium was originally written for the wedding of my longtime friend, Lisa Crooms. Without the eye and ear of another dear friend, Mendi Obadike, it would never have been fit for the occasion.

a question of survival: The poem responds to the news report from which this quote is taken: "It was the drugs that were making the children ill and the children had been enrolled on the secret trials without their relatives' or guardians' knowledge. . . . To be free in New York City,

you need money." Jamie Doran, "New York's HIV Experiment," http://news.bbc.co.uk/
2/hi/programmes/this_world/4038375.stm. The actual name of the nurse involved in the in-
famous Tuskeegee Experiment was Eunice Rivers, but I refer to her as "Evers," the name by
which she was called in the movie (and play) that dramatized this story and introduced it to
a wide, general audience.

soundtrack for a generational shift: This poem is in a modified acrostic form involving the first
words, rather than the first letters, of each line. The lyrics are from "The Composer," as
recorded by Diana Ross and the Supremes.

her table mountain: Before the city of Cape Town was established, the area around Table Moun-
tain, with its plentiful springs, streams, and fountains, was known as "Camissa," a Khoisan
word which loosely translates as "place of sweet waters." District Six was a racially mixed,
culturally vibrant community located in the middle of Cape Town. First, its black popula-
tion was forcibly removed very early in the 20th century; then, in 1966, the area was deemed
a "white area" under apartheid law, and authorities began displacing the 60,000 remaining
people of color (of varied ethnicities). When the displacement was complete (in 1982), the
buildings were all torn down and the area has remained almost entirely un(re)developed to
this day. My thanks to Patrick Gaspard, whose beautiful way with words jump-started (and
helped constitute) this poem.

acknowledgments

I would like to thank the editors of the following journals and anthologies for supporting my work by initially publishing (versions of) these poems:

1913: a journal of forms: "notes to my nieces" and "in a non-subjunctive mood"

Achiote Seeds: "the defense of marriage act, alternatives to," "a matter of balance," "bop for presidential politics, c. 2008," and "him/body/meant, her/body/meant"

Blue Fifth Review: "her tin skin" and "received in spring"

Cave Wall: "on new year's eve"

Carolina Quarterly: "revisiting"

Columbia Poetry Review: "celestial"

The Dead Mule School of Southern Literature: "riven"

Ecotone (Camille Dungy and Sebastian Matthews, special section editors): "her table mountain"

Ekleksographia (Amy King, guest editor): "clare's song" and "quiet as it's kept"

The Equalizer: "the cold"

Fingernails Across the Chalkboard: Poetry and Prose on HIV/AIDS from the Black Diaspora: "a question of survival"

Harvard Review: "owed to shirley chisholm :"

Indiana Review: "love life, with stitches"

La Petite Zine: "my last modernist poem, # 4 (or, re-re-birth of a nation)"

MELUS (Meta DuEwa Jones and Keith Leonard, guest editors): "never after"

No Tell Motel: "pink-think (a primer for girls of other colors)" and "salty (extended play)"

Oranges & Sardines (Poets & Artists): "at the musée de l'homme"

Pluck! The Journal of Affrilachian Arts & Culture: "a background in music"

PMS: poemmemoirstory (Honorée Fanonne Jeffers, special issue editor): "to see the minus"

Rainbow Darkness: An Anthology of African American Poetry: "from The Lost Letters of Frederick Douglass"

Sous Rature: "explosives," "you   can't deny it," and "x marks the spot"

The Southern Review: "a sonnet for stanley tookie williams" and "soundtrack for a generational shift"

Talisman (Joseph Donohue, guest editor): "my life as china" and "where's carolina?"

Tuesday; An Art Project: "statistical haiku (or, how do they discount us? let me count the ways)"

U.S. 1 Worksheets: "where you are planted"

I am grateful to the editors of these journals and anthologies for reprinting the following poems:

Black Nature: Four Centuries of African American Nature Poetry: "her table mountain"
The Dead Mule School of Southern Literature: "on new year's eve"
The Drunken Boat: "revisiting" and "where's carolina?"
MOTIF: Writing by Ear: "a background in music"
PoetryMagazine: "my life as china"

My thanks to the Center for Book Arts for producing a limited-edition broadside of "my life as china," beautifully designed and printed by Lindsay Valentin.

My thanks also to Chicago State University Theatre, which included "a question of survival" in the stage production based on the anthology *Fingernails Across the Chalkboard: Poetry and Prose from the Black Diaspora*, in which the poem first appeared.

Finally, there are a number of people—individuals and communities—who have led, pushed, or walked with me on this most recent stage of the journey. For nurturing the poet, a heartfelt thank you to the Cave Canem poets, the Squaw Valley Community of Writers, the stalwarts of the Lucipo listserv, the WomPo listserv, the women of Pussipo, and the Carolina African American Writers Collective. For inspiring poems, reading them, and offering honest feedback; for helping me wrestle the entire manuscript into shape; for calling my name; for saying *yes*; and for similar acts of love and goodwill that made this collection possible, I gratefully embrace Christian Campbell, Amy Sara Carroll, Joe Donohue, Camille Dungy, Cornelius Eady, Thomas Sayers Ellis, Danielle Evannou, Tonya Foster, C. S. Giscombe, Brenda Hillman, H. L. Hix, Leslieann Hobayan, Cathy Park Hong, Brandon Johnson, Tayari Jones, Amy King, Reb Livingston, Lenard D. Moore, Aldon Nielsen, Mendi Lewis Obadike, Danielle Pafunda, Sina Queyras, Howard Ramsby, Barbara Jane Reyes, Ed Roberson, Andrea Selch, and, of course, Suzanna Tamminen. I won't pretend that this exhausts the list but will carry on thanking many more people for their generosity for years to come.

And always, for everything, Stéphane Robolin.

evie shockley

is the author of *a half-red sea,* the chapbooks *31 words * prose poems* and *The Gorgon Goddess,* and the forthcoming study *Renegade Poetics: Black Aesthetics and Formal Innovation in African American Poetry.* She co-edits the literary journal *jubilat.* Originally from Nashville, Tennessee, she now lives in New Jersey, where she is an assistant professor of English at Rutgers University, New Brunswick.